SEVEN YEARS IN AFRICA.

LIBERIA AS IT IS.

BY

Rev. J. J. FITZGERALD,

MISSIONARY OF THE S. B. BOARD OF MISSIONS.

WE SPEAK THAT WE DO KNOW AND TESTIFY THAT WE HAVE SEEN.—*John* 3, 11 v.

COLUMBUS:
RICHARD NEVINS, PRINTER.
1866.

In the interest of creating a more extensive selection of rare historical book reprints, we have chosen to reproduce this title even though it may possibly have occasional imperfections such as missing and blurred pages, missing text, poor pictures, markings, dark backgrounds and other reproduction issues beyond our control. Because this work is culturally important, we have made it available as a part of our commitment to protecting, preserving and promoting the world's literature. Thank you for your understanding.

PREFACE.

Having resided nearly seven years in Liberia, engaged in the Missionary work, I have concluded to offer to the public the following account of the country, based upon my own personal observation and experience. I am the more constrained to do so, as I am continually being asked what kind of a country is the West African Republic.

It is to be regretted that those who have hitherto published accounts of the country, have either possessed insufficient information, obtained by a flying visit along the coast (in most instances not spending a single night on shore for fear of contracting the fever), or have been influenced by a desire to promote emigration, to give a one-sided and partial report of the land.

The object of the following chapters is to give the reader a true and impartial account of the country as it is, which my seven years' residence abundantly enables me to do.

Having been destitute of all support from the Board since 1861, in consequence of the American war, and having exhausted all of this world's goods that I possessed, when I gave myself to the work of missions, to sustain myself at my station and work during the last five years, and having returned to my native land destitute, with a family whose health is totally impaired by the climate of Africa, I hope, therefore, while this little work will convey to my friends and the public generally a correct impression of that land, so little known, it will also find sufficient sale to meet our present and pressing wants.

CHAPTER I.

CLIMATE, SOIL, SEASONS, ETC.

Liberia being situated between five and seven degrees north latitude, the sun is almost vertical at noon, and such is its intense heat from 10 o'clock A. M. till 4 P. M., that few persons can endure it without the constant use of an umbrella. Nevertheless, it is quite cool and pleasant in the shade. The sea breeze blows from 9 o'clock in the morning and cools the atmosphere, so that it is seldom sultry. The thermometer generally stands from 80 to 85 degrees in the shade; the nights are also cool, and to people who have the patience or indolence to keep in the shade, Liberia may be said to have a pleasant climate. The days and nights are about equal in length the year round. There is no evening or morning twilight; darkness and light succeed each other with a suddenness that is quite surprising.

There is little or no atmospheric phenomena in Liberia, nothing to compare with what may be seen in higher latitudes. There are no rosy tints or golden hues, morning or evening, but the sun rises and sets in a dull gray mist.

The year is divided into two seasons, called the wet and the dry season. The wet season commences about the middle of May and continues till the middle of November, during which time a vast quantity of rain falls. In the middle of the wet season the rain falls gradually and almost incessantly but in the beginning and latter part of the season the showers are more intermittent, and fall in sheets and torrents, accompanied with the most startling and terrific peals of thunder. There is something astonishing in the suddenness of these showers. One moment there is no indication of rain; the next instant it comes in torrents, flooding the streets, and again the next instant not a drop of rain is to be heard.

The thunder has the same habit of giving no warning of its approach, but bursts instantaneously upon you with terrific and startling power, crash following crash, and peal succeeding peal.

From the middle of November till the middle of May, is what is known as the dry season. In the commencement and ending of the dry season, there are occasional showers, but in the middle of the season there is frequently no rain for two or three months. Earth and sky glow with a fervid and oven-like appearance; vegetation is parched and crisped; water becomes scarce, and, in some localities, unattainable; animals look poor and languid, men feverish and irritable, and women fretful and peevish. Altogether this exceedingly dry and hot season is the most disagreeable of any in the year.

Liberia has 450 or 500 miles sea board. The soil can not be called rich or fertile when compared with the good lands of America. The natives never cultivate the same land two consecutive years, partly owing to its barrenness, and partly to their want of proper implements of husbandry. As a general rule, the land will not produce more than two years under American cultivation. The only exceptions are low clay lands.

There is no country in the world in which the farmer is liable to so many disappointments and bitter failures. Though there are no frosts or snows to rob him of the fruits of his toil, yet bugabugs, ants and other insects so infest the earth that they frequently devour what is planted before it has time to come up. The soil is deceptive. I do not hesitate to affirm that one acre of this country will go further and produce more for the maintenance of a family than five acres will in Western Africa.

The reports that have been circulated in this country of the wonderful productiveness of the African soil, are but a part of the thousand other misrepresentations resorted to to deceive the colored people of the United States, and to induce them to leave the land of their birth and emigrate to a pestilential climate, where, if fortunate enough to acclimate safely, they will at best, in a few years, sink into a premature grave. The soil is generally sandy, but clay exists in some localities, especially on the St. Paul's river, where bricks are made extensively.

The lands along the rivers and creeks are mostly mangrove swamps, and are subject to inundation at high tide, and emit a most offensive smell when the waters again recede.

One great hindrance to the development of the country is the want of interior navigation, and safe harbors on the sea board.

The rivers are not navigable for more than twenty or thirty miles, and that only for small boats and canoes, and the coast is destitute of natural harbors for the protection of shipping. Ships trading on the coast are compelled to anchor off outside, and there receive and discharge their cargoes. The cost of shipping is at least five hundred per cent. more than at Sierre Leone, and Sherbro, where there are good natural ports, without taking into account the loss of life, which is considerable. In this particular the Colonization Society made the worst possible selection as the site for their colony. No sane white men would ever have made such a choice for themselves, as a place to establish a new nationality, without a river navigable for ships or steamers, and without a harbor on the entire coast line.

The English, in selecting Sierre Leone and Sherbro, looked especially to these two particulars, so necessary and indispensable to the prosperity and development of all new countries, and chose two of the best natural harbors on the west coast of Africa. It is impossible, looking at the choice made by the agents of the Colonization Society, to resist the impression that they were providing for a people for whom they had no regard, and in whom they took no interest further than to remove them out of their sight.

Whatever opinion may be entertained of the good likely to result from the colonization movement, love to the colored race was no part of the motive that gave it being.

CHAPTER II.

PRODUCTIONS—METHOD OF CULTIVATION—PHYSICAL LABOR, ETC.

The productions of Liberia are similar to those of other tropical countries. The natives cultivate rice, cassava, corn, sweet potatoes, pumpkins, edoes, cucumbers, ground nuts and cotton. Rice and cassava being the principal food, are extensively cultivated; the other native productions receive but little attention. The colonists grow coffee, sugar, arrow root and ginger for exportation, and small quantities of corn, sweet potatoes and cassava for their own use. The coffee grown in Liberia has perhaps no superior in the world, and the sugar is of fair quality. Not being acquainted with the cultivation of sugar and coffee in other countries, I can not say whether the yield is large or small, but of other productions, such as corn, sweet potatoes, &c., five acres in Liberia will not produce as much as one acre of the good lands in America. Rice will not average more than ten bushels per acre, and corn less than rice; sweet potatoes not more than twenty-five or thirty. This will surprise many who have heard the soil of Liberia spoken of as of unsurpassed fertility, but I speak from actual knowledge and experience. I do not believe that more than ten bushels of corn have ever been produced from an acre of land in Liberia, from the first settlement of the colony to the present time.

The principal fruits are the orange, lemon, lime, sour-sop, sweet-sop, mangrove, plum, guava, pine-apple, plantain, banana, pa-paw, bread fruit, cocoanut and tamarind. Most of these need no description; with a few we will be more particular.

The sour-sop is a large fruit the size of a man's head. It has a rough green skin, the inner part of a snow white. It is pared, sliced and eaten with a little sugar. The pa-paw is of the size of the sour-sop, and resembles the musk-melon in color and taste, and is eaten with pepper and salt. The bread fruit is as large as either of the others, and is white and seedless. It is boiled or baked, and is very nutritious food. The butter fruit resembles the pear in color and size, and somewhat resembles fresh butter in taste.

Liberia has many and large fruits, some of which are truly delicious, but those who are used to the fruits of the temperate zones will always have a feeling of disappointment in exchanging them for the fruits of the tropics. Fruit, too, must be used with great moderation, as the too free indulgence in it is a prolific cause of disease in Africa.

METHOD OF CULTIVATION.

The bush (as the forests are generally called) consists of an impenetrable undergrowth, interspersed here and there with a few large trees. It is so thick that you can not see a dozen paces before you, except in spots unusually open. This bush is cut down during the dry season, and when it becomes perfectly dry it is set fire to, and the whole face of the land is burnt over, which, when well done, destroys the wild growth and the insects in the soil. The seed is then put in with the hoe. This is the only method of bringing new lands under cultivation. Great care must be taken that the bush is so cut that it will lie smooth all over the ground, that the fire may act on the entire surface. If the burn should be imperfect, it is quite useless to plant. Having no horses and but few oxen, the plow is never used. The only implement used for breaking up the soil is the hoe. It may be thought that this shows a want of enterprise, but I do not believe that the plow can be used to advantage in Liberia, for neither horses (if they could live, which they can not in that climate) nor oxen could possibly draw the plow and live one season.

In this connection I may as well speak of the effects of the climate upon physical labor. Neither man nor beast can perform one-third of the work in Africa that they could in America. I have no doubt that three months work, such as is ordinarily performed on an American farm, would, in the majority of cases, result in death if done in Liberia.

A native of Africa cannot do as much work in his own climate as an American can do at home. Native laborers will work ten hours a day and at the same time he will not accomplish as much work as could be done elsewhere in five hours. It is useless to attempt to get more out of him, the climate does not permit it. If you force him beyond his strength in a few days he is on the sick list, and your farm without hands. I have often over-worked myself to accomplish a given amount by a given time, and the result was always the same —an attack of fever that compelled me to lay by from all labor for a time. I never, during seven years' residence in Africa, could do one-third of the work that I could have done in this country without the least injury. It may be asked do not some of the Liberians exceed this ratio of labor; I answer, they do and they kill themselves by it. Instances of men killing themselves by working above their strength are not few or far between.

There is no place where poor people who are compelled to toil for the necessaries of life, live so short a time and have so hopeless an existence. People who are able to provide the necessaries and some of the comforts of life, such as proper food and clothing, good residences, &c., if they are temperate and fortunate in their acclimation may hope to live a somewhat shorter life than in their native land. But if they are poor and dependent on their daily or monthly wages, and are consequently deprived of the necessaries of life, as they must be if dependent on their own labor (as we shall show in another chapter) a very few years, in the majority of cases, will close their earthly exisistence. No man has half the strength after he has had the African fever that he had before. I am conscious that the utterance of such facts as the above, will kindlethe hatred of those against me who have been suppressing these facts from the colored people. But knowing them as I do, I should not feel innocent of blood guiltiness if I were to pass over them in silence. Neither can I virtually tell a lie by suppressing the truth and by my silence sanction and endorse the thousand deceptions that have been practised upon my race.

CHAPTER III.

AFRICAN FEVER—CAUSE AND EFFECTS—ACCLIMATION, ETC.

African fever is the great enemy that persons have to encounter who go to Africa to reside. It is the great obstacle to its civilization and christianization. It has ever been the chief hindrance to successful enterprise and the internal development of the country. On no other principle can we account for the fact that Africa, settled shortly after the flood and known to the ancients, still remains a sealed region, a terraincognita.

The barriers of eternal snow, and the icy hills that environ the arctic regions, have in vain attempted to arrest the progress of that spirit of daring enterprise and wild adventure, that has accomplished so many wonders iu the last four centuries.

The most remote islands of the deep have been discovered and explored. A new world, unknown to the ancients in the far west, has been brought under the charm of civilization, its majestic forests have disappeared as by magic, and in their stead cities and towns have sprung up as by enchantment.

But Africa, occupying a central position on the globe, lying in the great highway of commerce, rich in natural resources, is still undeveloped and unknown. Enterprise and adventure have stopped at the threshold of this mysterious region and dared not enter its secret shades. The only cause that can be assigned for this is the malignity of its climate. But for this the interior of that great land would have been as well known as that of Europe, the resources of the country developed, her commerce would glut the market of the world, and the gold mines of Senegambia would be as familiar as those of California. Permanent civilization would have been inaugurated where now the native builds his mud house as he did twenty centuries ago.

The African fever is caused by the miasma or malaria arising from its low lands and mangrove swamps, in which there is in continual process of decay, vast quantities of vegetable matter. The rivers are margined by great swamps and in the wet season millions of acres of land are overflown which are perfectly dry the remainder of the year. Large rivers sweep along where at other seasons there is no water.

I have traveled fifty or sixty miles in the month of July in boats and canoes across the country through fields and forests where, for six months of the year, there is scarcely water enough to drink. These vast quantities of vegetable growth alternately exposed to the heat of the sun, and the water causing the most rapid decomposition, together with the great heat of the climate, accounts for the existence of malaria, the great and prolific cause of African fever.

The first attacks of fever generally commence after two or three months' residence, though some persons escape for six, nine and twelve months. The fever generally comes on with severe chills succeeded with burning fever and in favorable types goes off with profuse perspiration. Persons going through this process of acclimation during an attack usually have the fever once a day, but frequently twice and thrice a day. The fever often produces delirium—the patient not recognizing his own family. It has a most depressing effect upon the mind, producing gloom, despondency and despair.

The attacks, when favorable, generally last from two to four weeks, and recur at short intervals for two or three years, when they become less frequent and violent.

The constitution being stronger at first arrival in Africa than at any subsequent period, it has greater power to resist and throw off the fever, and to recover from the disease than it has after it has been reduced by repeated attacks; hence, the fever is not so prostrating and debilitating in its earlier stage as it is after a residence of twelve or eighteen months.

The opinion is general in America that the ordeal of acclimation is complete or nearly so in six months; so far is this from the truth that in most cases it has scarcely begun, and in all the most trying period is still to be passed.

When the fever does not at once assume a malignant and deadly form (which it sometimes does,) the first six months is the least dangerous period in the process.

Properly speaking, acclimation is never complete, the spells of fever become less frequent and malignant after two or three years, but there will be returns of fever during life. People from the temperate zones can never enjoy the strength and health in Africa as elsewhere. At no time, in Africa, could I do one-third of the work that I could have done in America. Such is the African fever, as a general rule.

There are some exceptions that we will now consider:

The fever sometimes assumes at once the most malignant and deadly form, yields to no treatment, and kills swift and surely. At other times it takes a milder form, but wastes away the strength by slow, continual fevers, till the patient, without seeming very ill, sinks into the grave. A very few persons have but little or no fever at all. Those who pass through the African fever successfully do so with impaired constitutions and greatly reduced strength. It is a singular fact that the fever is quite as deadly to animals as men. Horses, dogs, mules, &c., imported into the country soon die. Attempts have been made to get horses from other tropical lands, and from the interior of Africa, but none of those imported from these countries withstood the climate of the coast. Another great mistake exists relative to the African fever, and the sooner it is exploded the better. It is thought that it is less fatal to colored people than to whites; that the colored people of the United States can live in Liberia, and that white people cannot. This is as contrary to facts as it is to reason, and it is astonishing that the advocates of colonization continue to make such declarations, knowing as some of them do, that there is not a shadow of truth in them. There are many white people in Liberia, Sierra Leone and Sherbro, who are merchants, missionaries, clerks, &c., and the mortality and sickness among them is not greater than that of the American colonist. In Sierra Leone there are one hundred whites, at Sherbro twenty-five, and a number in Liberia, and I have remarked that they seem to suffer less from fever than the emigrants from the United States, and I attribute it to the fact that, generally, they are better provided for.

But let us turn from mere assertion to a few facts and figures showing the mortality of the two classes. The Mindi Mission, in the Sherbro country, has been operating twenty-five years, and have had in employ about forty-five white missionaries, male and female, of which fourteen have died during their missionary labors in Africa, or about thirty-one per cent. But few of these forty-five missionaries were ever at the mission at any one time, and all of them returned home to recruit every three or four years. It would, therefore, be equivalent, perhaps, to forty-five missionaries for seven years constant service, or four and one-half per cent. of deaths among them annually. On the other hand the Waters family emigrated to Liberia about the year 1856, numbering forty-five persons. In 1865, nine years, there was but seven of them alive, a mortality of eighty-five per cent. in nine years, a little more than nine per cent. yearly, double that of the white missionaries on the Sherbro. But again, the Mount Zion Baptist Church, at Cape Mount, of one hundred and six members, at its most prosperous period, lost, by death, in two years, eighteen members, or nine per cent. annually, without epidemic or any unusual cause of mortality, and all of them acclimated persons except myself and wife. Both of these two instances are taken from Cape Mount, the most celebrated for health of any settlement in Liberia, and are sufficient to convince every candid mind that the climate is as deadly to colored people as to whites, all things being equal. Why, then, is it said and believed by honest people, that the black man can live there but the white man can not? It is because the Colonization Society has so often affirmed it that many have taken it for the truth without investigation. Their great object is to remove the colored people from this country, and though thousands perish, they falter not. It is an undeniable fact that, in the earlier days of the colony, as high as fifty and seventy-five per cent. perished the first year after landing, and in some cases nearly the whole ship load died. Yet the Colonization Society never faltered in their work of death, but sent ship load after ship load over to no other inheritance than an African grave.

The idea that the colored people who, for generations, have lived in America, and are as perfectly adapted to the climate as the white people (simply because their ancestors some ten or fifteen generations ago, came from Africa,) can endure the climate one whit better than the whites, is simply absurd and as contrary to reason and common sense as it is to facts. Native Africans, who are absent for a few years, on returning to Africa have the African fever; how much more those who left the country ten generations ago in the loins of their ancestors!

CHAPTER IV.

POPULATION, CUSTOMS, CONDITION, ETC., ETC.

The population of Liberia is variously estimated at from twelve to fifteen thousand, but either of these estimates I think is too large. It does not exceed ten thousand or ten thousand five hundred. There is also a native population of eighty thousand within the territory claimed by the Government, but over a greater part of which they exercise no kind of jurisdiction. The natives, with the exception of those in the immediate neighborhood of the civilized settlements, pay not the slightest regard to the government or its laws, and are as independent of Liberia as they are of Egypt. There is no place on the coast of Liberia, Monrovia excepted, where the laws of the republic can be enforced ten miles from the sea board, and generally not five miles. Liberia has six settlements scattered along four hundred miles of sea board—Cape Mount, Monrovia, Junk, Bassa, Sinoo and Palmas. Along the coast between these settlements the native rule is complete. Americans going among them must conform to, and be governed by, the native laws. It is a fact that the Liberian Government can not, or do not, protect its citizens in passing between these settlements. Boats and vessels wrecked between ports are robbed by the natives with impunity.

A few of the Liberians are wealthy merchants or well to do farmers, but the great mass are helplessly and hopelessly poor. I have never seen, in any other country, such general and extreme poverty. Nor does it arise from laziness or intemperate habits, but from the fact that the supply of labor greatly exceeds the demand. The American laborer is brought in competition with native labor that can be obtained at three dollars per month. Good foremen on a farm do not command more than six and eight dollars per month. A laborer's wages will not sustain life in a comfortable manner in Liberia, unless he has some capital to commence business on his own account. If dependent on his daily or monthly wages, he has nothing before him but to drag out a short and miserable existence, unworthy the name of life, of hopeless, abject poverty and pinching want. The next question is, how are his wages paid. If his four, five, six or eight dollars were paid in specie, and he could buy his supplies at the cheapest market, it would be some advantage to the poorer class; but he receives his wages in cloth, leaf tobacco, rice, pork and any such articles as he may need; common calico at forty and fifty cents per yard, leaf tobacco at seventy-five cents per pound, and other articles at similar rates.

This is the almost universal manner of paying for labor. No laborer can clothe himself decently, much less support a family, out of the proceeds of his labor in Liberia.

What possible chance have the poor people landed penniless, under such circumstances, to accumulate any thing?

Female labor commands from two to two and a half dollars per month; washing twenty-five cents per day.

Two months' wages are required to pay for one pair of shoes, and if the poor woman should wear three pair in the year, one-half of the year's wages must go to pay for them; and if she works the whole year, she has but twelve dollars to meet all her other wants.

Look at these facts, and it will be seen that the great mass of bare-footed and ragged people of Liberia are not so from indolence, but necessity. The wealthy class live in a style superior to people of the same means in America. They have elegant houses, expensive furniture and many servants. A servant attends them when shopping or at market, to take home anything they may purchase. Such is their foolish pride that it is considered disgraceful to be seen carrying anything through the streets. They drink coffee early in the morning, breakfast at ten o'clock A. M., dine at five o'clock P. M., and take tea before retiring. Such are the customs of the wealthier class. The poor people eat only twice in the day—at ten o'clock A. M. and five o'clock P. M., and are glad then to have something to appease hunger.

There are some vices to which the people are not much addicted. Drunkenness is seldom seen except on days of election, when the opposing candidates or their friends provide free whisky or rum, which is freely drank in honor of liberty and Liberia.

Profanity is also unusual. This unmanly vice, for which there is less excuse than for almost any other, is less indulged in by the Liberians than any equal number of people almost anywhere else. Duelling is almost unknown. Challenges are sometimes given and accepted, but the parties generally manage, by writing their wills, engaging their coffins and other sentimental conduct, to let the authorities into the secret, so that they may interpose and prevent the shedding of blood.

Nevertheless, the Liberians are not a people of superior morality. Their vices are of a different kind. There is a want of principle, of common honesty and truth in their dealings. The lowest and basest villainy, consummated by falsehood and duplicity, is called sharpness, shrewdness and ability. The violation of every pledge and the most sacred obligations of gratitude and honor, if a temporary advantage can be gained thereby, far from branding the doer with infamy, is considered a distinguishing mark of cleverness. This want of truth and honesty is the great sin of the land; hence, reports, statistics, state papers, &c., are, in many instances, greatly exaggerated or utterly untrue. I have been told, when speaking of these inaccuracies, that they were meant to be read abroad. No one who has not lived in Liberia can have the least conception of the little reliance to be placed upon publications emanating from Liberia.

There is nothing that shows the depravity of a community more than the frequency of divorce. Liberia is the land of divorces. That they are shamefully and alarmingly common, the records of the court and the journals of legislation abundantly show. When the courts can not meet all the demands made upon them by unhappy families who are anxious to form other connexions, the Legislature comes to their aid, often passing three or four divorse bills during a single session.

What stamps this immorality with a deeper enormity is, that a woman, when divorced from one man, soon marries another; and, in many instances, it is evidently a prearrangement.

Of the chastity of Liberian society I forbear to speak. In all countries where the female element greatly exceeds the male, where the supply of labor greatly exceeds the demand, there is always a multitude of females unprovided for, whose penury is often taken advantage of. Such a state of society is unfavorable to virtue. Perhaps no country of the same population has so many widows and unmarried females. Being less exposed to the weather they stand the climate better than men. Hence widows and other destitute unmarried females are abundant, and the state of society is such as may be expected under the circumstances. It must be remembered that the most of the Liberians are from the South or descended from Southern parents, and their vices are such as slavery has entailed upon them.

Yet there are many good and excellent people in Liberia. It is but just to say that they have some good scholars, men of thorough business capacity, lawyers of respectable ability, and physicians of good skill.

CHAPTER V.

INDUCEMENTS TO EMIGRANTS—HOW RECEIVED, ETC.

Like all other countries, Liberia has its advantages and disadvantages as a place of residence. We will present them in this chapter as faithfully as our knowledge of the country will enable us to do, and leave the reader to judge on which side the balance belongs.

Liberia has no long winter to consume the earnings of the summer.

Less expense need be incurred for fuel and heavy clothing than in lands where

> "Through woods and mountain passes
> The winds like anthems roll."

Labor can be employed at from three to five dollars per month, and native servants can be had for feeding and clothing them. Their food and clothing will not cost more than eight dollars a year. One quart of rice and a little oil is the daily allowance for a servant, and six yards of calico will clothe him in the ordinary style. The government is republican. The President, Vice President, Senators and Representatives are elected by the people. All the other officers of the government down to a petty constable are appointed by the President, and hold office during his good pleasure.

Land is cheap and abundant, and by having high and low land something may be produced the greater part of the year.

These are some of the peculiar advantages of Liberia. On the other hand, there are many and grave disadvantages in the way of making it a home.

The following extract, taken from the "Early Dawn," a paper published by the Mindi Mission, at Sherbro, West Africa, not only vividly presents the disadvantages the colored people must encounter in settling in Liberia, but confirms and endorses much that we have elsewhere written:

"Africa has a great surplus of laborers. They throng our trading posts and mission stations, anxious to work for the barest pittance of pay, and content to live on what would be wholly inadequate to support an American laborer. The price of labor in Africa is fifteen shillings per month, and a quart of rice daily. The price of labor in America is about four times as great; while the cost of comfortable houses, clothing, &c., is not half so great as in Africa.

"The colored people of America are almost without exception natives of that country. They can endure this climate but little if any better than white people. A large per centage of those who come here die in acclimation, and of those who survive the per centage of deaths is about equal to that of births. We can scarcely conceive of a more miserable condition, than for a laboring man thrown upon this coast without a knowledge of the climate, and unable to procure the comforts of civilization. There are about twelve millions of African people in North and South America and the West Indies. These are the descendants of about twelve millions of slaves which have been sent from the coast of Africa. Of this twelve millions at least eight millions must have died in consequence of their being taken from their native land, and we believe that if it were possible to transport the twelve millions of colored Americans to Africa it would result in a similar loss of life. We believe, therefore, in Africa, for the Africans, and that they who advocate any scheme of African colonization by Americans, are but playing into the hands of the haters and oppressors of the African race."

There are three things in this extract, from the pen of a white missionary who lived in Africa a number of years, and was well acquainted with African life, to which we invite especial attention: The great surplus of labor, the malignity of the climate, and its equally fatal effects upon the colored people as upon the whites. Does a country where thousands of laborers can be obtained at fifteen shillings per month, or three dollars and sixty cents, offer any great inducement to leave a country where labor costs more than fifteen dollars per month, to a people who are mostly poor and dependent upon the labor of their hands? The friends of African colonization tell us that there we will enjoy perfect equality and freedom; and in the sacred name of that freedom they deny us here, they cajole and entice the colored people to that land of pestilence and death. But does the emigrant enjoy that equality on his arrival that he is promised? I answer, no! I put the question to any man's common sense, can a people, who are hopelessly poor and dependent on a few richer and older residents for employment, (at wages that will not clothe them in the most ordinary manner,) be free and independent? Can any man be free when pinching want enslaves him to the will of another? Can any civilized man labor at three dollars and sixty cents per month without being hopelessly dependent on his employer? The answer to these questions are self-evident and obvious. This leads us to consider how emigrants are received and regarded by the old settlers. That there is a strong prejudice against the emigrant or (new comer, as he is called,) can not be denied. The term *new comer* is one of reproach, and the *new comer* is considered a bird that every old settler has a right to pick till he is featherless. Thefts, extortions, robberies, lawsuits, &c., &c., are all resorted to to relieve him of his money, and they generally succeed in their kind intentions. The great object seems to be to reduce him to beggary, which they facetiously call *making him pay his footing in the country*. I have known men to arrive in Liberia with several thousand dollars, in goods and cash, and in two or three years the same men, by thefts, malicious suits, extortions, &c., were reduced to beggary. Mr. Dent, who emigrated from the State of Georgia, was a pious, industrious, enterprising and strictly honest man, who brought with him several thousand dollars, and this man, who would have made his way in any part of the world, was, in three years, brought to utter destitution in the manner I have described.

These cases are so common that it has become a saying in Liberia, "that a man of means must first lose all that he has," and they seldom fail to make the saying true.

If the emigrant shows the least indignation at these displays of their intellectual ability (for such they call it) he awakes a storm from all the old land sharks who claim the right to eat all the smaller fish. To call these intellectual displays by such names as villany, rascality, or dishonesty, subjects the new-comer to a suit for slander, from which he need not hope to escape without paying heavy damages for being so imprudent as to call things by their proper names. At the same time it is the most difficult thing for him to obtain redress for any wrongs done him by the old settlers. Right or wrong, the new-comer must pay his footing in the country. It may be asked, do not the Liberians want emigration to their country? Yes, above everything else. Every new emigration affords them more subjects on which to exercise their peculiar talents, and a new field in which to reap where they have not sown.

One object of the people is to reduce the means of the emigrant so that he will never be able to leave the country. Every means is adopted to prevent his return. I am often asked, " with your present knowledge would you go to Liberia, or would you conscientiously recommend others to do so?" I answer, "Africa is the land of our ancestors, and if any colored man is willing to sacrifice his own ease, comfort and convenience, encounter the dangers of the climate, and suffer the privations incident to a residence in that land, and devote himself to its elevation, I would bid him God-speed." To engage in this great and noble work, I would gladly see many competent colored christians go—

"Where Afric's sunny fountains
Roll down their golden sand."

Men of capital, who are willing to assist in the renovation of their fatherland by the extention of commerce and agriculture, I would recommend to go to that wide field of enterprise. But to recommend it as a home, to the mass of the American people of color, would be to stain my hands with the blood of those whom I would thus deceive and betray to a premature grave.

The suffering, destitution and death that I have seen among the widows and orphans and poor is truly revolting, and to send ship loads of destitute freedmen to Liberia is, in my opinion, but little better than wholesale murder.

CHAPTER VI.

ANIMALS, BIRDS, REPTILES, INSECTS, ETC.

Liberia, like other tropical countries, is most prolific in animal life. Nature seems to have indulged her wildest whims in producing animals, reptiles, and insects, of almost endless variety, and some of prodigious size. There are in the country six different species of deer, they all have straight, short horns. The gazelle is small, weighing about ten pounds, and of a mouse color. The water deer is of similar size, and the skin is beautifully variegated with white spots. On the least alarm this deer plunges into the water and swims, and dives with an expertness that baffles all pursuit. The black and red deer are as large as those of America. The mountain deer is of small size, and the skin has jet black stripes running across the back.

Large droves of wild hogs roam in the bush. Some of the boars attain an immense size, and are armed with large tusks. They are truly a formidable and ferocious animal. There are many varieties of monkeys, which differ in size and color.

There is the black monkey, the blue monkey, the lion monkey, the mangrove monkey, and the small grey monkey. The lion monkey has a mane resembling the lion. The king monkey has a white ring around the neck, and seems to exercise some kind of supremacy over the rest, for when he utters his voice, all others keep the most profound silence. Monkeys, in whatever they are engaged, always keep a sentinel on guard, who, on the least approach of danger, sounds a sharp cry of alarm, when, as if by magic, every monkey disappears. It is said by the natives that if a monkey is injured through the neglect of the sentinel, before the alarm is given, the rest fall immediately upon him and kill him. The Chipanzee abounds in the Cape Mount region. It stands, when erect, from five feet to five feet five inches high. It beats on its breast, making a deep bass drumming sound, and such is its wonderful strength that in its vice-like grasp it can twist and double the barrel of a gun. The natives fear this animal more than any other in the country. It has immense muscles, and wheighs, when full grown, from 150 to 175 pounds. They go in pairs and the females carry their young upon their back.*

Wild cows are numerous, and very ferocious; when wounded they never fail to charge their assailants with headlong fury. They are, perhaps, the most malignant antagonists to be met with in the Liberian forests. The water cow and hippopotamus exists in some of the rivers; when attacked and wounded they charge their assailants with the utmost fury, and woe to the hunter who has not shelter from these assaults. Leopards are common in all parts of the country, but are not as dangerous as generally supposed—seldom attacking men unless wounded, in which case they are most relentless. Elephants, the largest of all quadrupeds, are abundant, and are the lords of the forest.

There are birds of almost endless variety, the guinea-fowl, the pea-fowl, and parrots are abundant in the African forests. There are many poisonous snakes and other reptiles in Liberia. The largest snake is the boa constrictor, which often attain a length of twenty-five or thirty feet, and are able to crush a large deer and swallow it. The bite of the boa constrictor is not poisonous. He crushes his prey in his coils. A most superb and beautiful snake of this kind lived in a large bugabug hill, on some land which I cultivated, at Cape Mount. I saw him frequently, and on two occasions when he seemed indisposed to yield the path. Assisted by several of my laborers I attacked him, taking good care to decline any embrace that his snakeship might be disposed to give me. After a slight resistance he ascended a large tree with great

---

* This animal, called the Chimpangee in Liberia, differs very much from those on other parts of the coast of the same name, and are of more than three times the size of some that I saw at Sherbro and Sierra Leone.

rapidity. This snake was such a superb creature that I was much attached to it, and intended some day to capture him alive, but one of my neighbors, to whom I pointed out his retreat, afterwards shot him, to my great disgust. The cassava snake has a blunt tail, which he seems to regard with especial pride, and will not bite, though you walk all over his body, till you touch his tail, when he strikes instantly, and kills with the certainty of a rifle ball.

The natives, who have many strange stories, tell one of this snake. They say that he had a most excellent disposition till God cut off his tail, and that it has been sore ever since, and that hence he bites only those who touch it. Black and green snakes are also common, but I do not think that snakes are more abundant than in America. Claw scorpions, are a dangerous reptile, that live about the house, concealing themselves in crevices, and in clothes, and bed-quilts, &c. Their bite is sometimes fatal. Alligators abound in all the rivers, some are of immense size. People are frequently carried off by them. While I lived in Cape Mount three of the inhabitants were carried off by an alligator that lurked about the place, and though he was frequently shot, all attempts to kill him proved abortive.

I shall only name two of the numerous kinds of insects that infest the land. The drivers are a kind of large black ant that live in communities of countless millions, under the direction of a king. They put every living thing to flight in their march, and are days passing any given point. When they come to a house in their march they never leave it till every room, closet, nook, corner and crevice is taken possession of, and completely searched; when this is accomplished they fall in line, and in a few moments retire from the premises. It is useless to attempt to beat them off, they come again and again, attacking from all points of the compass till the place is carried. Their visits must be regarded as a blessing as they drive away all other poisonous reptiles and insects. They often cross streams of water, the larger and stronger fastening themselves together by their claws, thus forming a bridge for the smaller and weaker. The bugabug is an insect that builds a house or ant hill, ten or twelve feet high, in which they have chambers, halls, a king's palace, and everything convenient for the community.

The space we have assigned for these chapters compel us to omit an account of many interesting animals and insects.

Was it not for the climate Liberia would be the paradise of hunters. Elephants, wild cows, leopards, chimpanzees, wild boars, water cows, hippopotamus, would afford sport and adventure for the most daring, while guinea-fowls, pea-fowls, pheasants and deer would delight the epicure.

CHAPTER VII.

DISEASES OF THE CLIMATE—SCRAPS AND FRAGMENTS.

African fever is not the only dangerous disease prevalent in Liberia. Very singularly, considering the mildness of the climate, consumption is common, and a most deadly disorder. Diarrhœa is also, in that climate, a dreadful and deadly complaint, but, if treated in time, yields more readily than consumption. Ulcerated feet and ankles is a prevalent, painful, loathesome and fatal malady. The feet swell to double the ordinary size, while a large ulcer, the size of a man's hand, is continually running. They are exceedingly hard to cure, often remaining for years. If healed suddenly they prove fatal. The only way to deal with them is to heal them very slowly. The scratch of a pin or brier will often produce one of these frightful ulcers, which will be years in healing, or result in death. Leprosy exists there, but is unfrequent. Dropsy is a common disease, which is seldom cured; but the most singular of all is the sleepy disease. Persons having this malady become so irresistibly inclined to slumber that they fall asleep while eating or while engaged at their daily business. They have no pain except when roused up, when the effort to wake seems to be painful. The disease finally gets the mastery, and it is impossible to wake them. They sleep on till, without pain or consciousness, they expire. No cure for this malady has yet been discovered. When the disease has once commenced death is the consequence.

The crawcraw is a disease of the skin, not dangerous, but exceedingly annoying. Not only people, but animals of all descriptions, have this disease.

The chief articles of export are palm oil, cam wood and ivory, and small quantities of coffee and sugar.

There is native iron in the interior of excellent quality, of which the natives manufacture their implements of husbandry and war. The palm tree is perhaps the most useful tree in Liberia or in the world. From it the natives obtain oil, wine, cabbage, turnips and a strong fibre.

It may be asked, "Has Liberia exerted an influence for good upon the native tribes?" I answer, the influence of Liberia has been one of a mixed character, for good and evil. While she has not done all that is sometimes claimed for her, she has doubtless done something for the christianization and more for the civilization of that part of the coast. She doubtless in time will be the means of doing immense good to that dear land. To claim that Liberia has caused the abolition of the slave trade for five or six hundred miles of sea board is simply absurd. Were it not for English influence and English men of war on the coast, the slave trade would not only exist between ports, but in the lesser ports of the republic themselves.

The government has not the power to prevent the natives trading in slaves, if the English men of war did not keep the slaves off the coast.

I would add, in conclusion of this chapter, that in Africa I feel a deep and abiding interest. As a field of Christian and missionary enterprise, I recommend it to all who are willing to spend and be spent in the cause of her elevation, counting not their lives dear. Why should we not make the sacrifice? Why should white missionaries be the instrumentality of the redemption of our fatherland? All things being equal, colored missionaries will be more successful than white ones.

As a general rule, a missionary of the same race and color of those to whom he is sent will be more successful than one of a different race. Christ himself, as a Hebrew, confined his personal ministry to the lost sheep of the House of Israel, and said that he was sent to none else as far as his personal labors were concerned. Had I the interest and welfare of none other than myself to consult, I should certainly return to Africa, and devote myself, in some way, to its welfare.

All that I have written of Liberia that is unfavorable, has been written in submission to truth. I should have been glad to have recorded only what was good and worthy of praise.

That these chapters may convey to the public a more correct impression of Liberia than has hitherto been made by reports, some of them ignorantly and some designedly, wishing to deceive them, is the earnest wish of the author.

CHAPTER VIII.

NATIVE TRIBES—CUSTOMS, CHARACTER AND HABITS.

There are many native tribes in Liberia, among which are the Veys, Gollas, Bassas, Krooman, Mandingoes and others. It is a mistake to suppose the native Africans are all or mostly black; on the contrary, a pure black complexion in many tribes is the exception and not the general rule. The Veys and Mandingoes are mostly of a brown complexion. I had prepared my mind when I went to Africa to see an ugly, debased people, with very heavy features and low, receding foreheads. But these are not the characteristics of the African at home. In all of these particulars I was so much surprised that I could scarcely believe that I was in Africa, and among the people that I had so often seen represented in American geographies and missionary journals. While these people's features are not as sharp as the American's, they are still further from being the thick-lipped, flat-nosed race represented in American prints. With regard to their feet and hands I do not hesitate to say that they are smaller and handsomer than the educated class of American white people. The low and receding forehead is not found among the native tribes of Liberia. I have often remarked the superiority of the natives in this respect to the colonists from America. These traits, as seen in the colored people of America, must be charged to the account of four centuries of oppression and slavery. For well developed heads I do not hesitate to say that the Veys, Maringoes and Gollas, equal the less educated people of Europe and America.

I was also surprised at the independent and self-possessed appearance and bearing of the natives. There is nothing slavish or cringing in their manner; on the contrary, they are bold, defiant and independent, tenacious of their rights, and not cowardly in defending them.

The following extract, taken from a work entitled Crime and Injustice, published at London, illustrates the character of the native African:

"About thirty years ago a British force, sent to the Gold Coast to chastise the King of Ashantee, was disastrously defeated, and its general, Sir Charles Macartney, killed by that prince. In our own times we have had a governor of the Gambier severely trounced, and nearly tarred and feathered, by a tribe of disdainful and humorsome negroes up that river. At Lagos, some three years ago, an expedition was repulsed and driven out of it with considerable loss, by a black monarch whom it went up to depose, at the instance of the Church missionaries settled there and at Abeokuta, who desired to set up in his stead a rum-drinking and otherwise spiritually disposed friend of their own, given however, as it turned out, to slave-dealing as well as strong waters. And now we have been defeated in an expedition up a river near Sierra Leone. But no doubt we have some military successes to set against these misfortunes, and to rectify the balance of 'glory' in western Africa. Such, for instance, as the destruction the other day of a native town up the Old Calabar, 'at,' said Sir Charles Wood, 'the request of the missionaries,' though why or wherefore those reverend gentlemen should have exacted such vengeance the First Lord of the Admiralty could not tell the House of Commons. But whether our assaults be successful or unsuccessful matters little to commerce, for with the negroes chastisement has very little effect to alter their conduct, and success on their part never provokes them into retaliation. The truth is, of all God's creatures (Yankees not excepted) the negro is perhaps the most commercially disposed of mankind. Whether you blow his brains out, or he knocks you on the head, he is equally ready and willing to trade with you the next day, as this last affair abundantly testifies. But then he is not to be dragooned out of his opinion, or to be attacked with impunity. He is obstinate in his own view of his 'rights,' and valiant against all apparent odds in defense of his home and his property, as we shall see.

"Governor Kennedy, of Sierra Leone, is now in Europe on an unusually prolonged leave of absence, and in his place there reigneth as acting governor a colored gentleman, desirous, it would seem, to distinguish himself, but with small discretion and little wit. Shortly after Governor Kennedy's departure, he sent a large expedition, consisting of three ships of war and nearly 500 troops, up one of the rivers opposite the peninsula of Sierra Leone. This expedition at once came to terms with the refractory Chief of Mallaghea, Bamba Mimah Lahi, who, desirous to get rid of so overwhelming a force from before his town, agreed to pay in the March following 1,000 dollars, by way of indemnity for his alleged offenses; as of course he would have promised, under such pressure, to pay a million, had it been demanded. March came round, but not the money. The negro chief offered 300 dollars, but the acting governor refused that sum, and in May sent a small expedition, consisting of only one ship of war and 150 rank and file, to enforce payment of the difference in dispute—namely 700 dollars. When this expedition reached Mallaghea some negotiations took place; the chief either not having, or pretending not to have, a thousand dollars in hand. The expedition, directed by an inferior clerk in the government office at Freetown, insisted on full payment; and in a letter written by a merchant on the spot, it is stated that at last 'the king had sent the whole of the money, say 1,030 dollars, to Binty, requesting Mr. Davidson to receive it in behalf of government, but that gentleman refused to receive it.' However this was, on the 23d of May the ship opened fire on the town, and it was quickly in flames, night only closing on the bombardment. Nevertheless, next day, a portion of the town was seen still standing; and the rockets proving worthless, just as in the Ashantee war kegs of macaroni instead of gunpowder were brought into action, the troops were landed ignobly armed, as we read, with lucifer matches, to ignite the standing remnant of the place; but from behind the smoking ruins they received so murderous a negro fire that, after seventy-three killed, wounded and missing, they fled to the ship, and got back to Sierra Leone with all possible despatch."

Naturally they are a kind, hospitable people. The life of a stranger is sacred in time of peace, where they have not been brutalized by the slave trade. I always felt the most perfect security among them while sleeping in their interior towns, with nothing more secure to my door than a common country cloth. I knew that there was not a murderous heart among them, wild as they were, and that life was perfectly secure in time of peace, when proper regard was shown to their laws. They do not soon forget injuries, and will sometimes go to war to revenge wrongs done to their ancestors.

The African kings, or the more powerful of them, such as Prince Mand, King Buoyer, and others, compel the most punctilious respect from the English and Americans that enter their dominions. Such is the willing obedience of their subjects, that a stranger who offended the king would be denied a cup of water or a mouthful of food by the entire tribe, at the command of the king.

The King of Ashantee, in the war with the English and their confederates on the coast, was entirely victorious, defeating the allies and invading their territory with thirty thousand troops. Prince Mand is a wealthy man, has an army well supplied with arms, powder and cannon, and not only an abundance of silver spoons, forks and knives, but silver pitchers, soup tureens, wash bowls, goblets, &c. He has a prison and chain gang for criminals, and more than three hundred wives. He is truly a princely African, and rules his country with a strong hand.

The natives are large cultivators of the soil, and are truly an agricultural people. Hundreds of acres may be seen in a single rice farm, and I think that not less than thirty thousand bushels of rice can be bought in a season at Cape Mount alone.

They manufacture country cloths from the native cotton, and are expert workmen in iron, silver, and gold; yet, these people are called savages and are supposed to subsist on snakes, snales, &c., when the truth is, that they not only have plenty for themselves, but supply all the civilized settlements of Sierra Leone, Sherbro, and Liberia, and the vessels trading on the coast, with food.

DOMESTIC SLAVERY.

The domestic slavery existing among them is scarcely worthy of the name, and is not what is understood by that term in America. It more nearly resembles the old patriarchal system of servitude. The master is called the father and the servants are regarded as his children. He performs such duties for the master, as long established custom has sanctioned as his duty, and the balance of his time is his own. He cultivates a farm of his own, and sells the produce to whom he pleases. What he does is without compulsion, or overseeing, and the master's slaves compose his army in time of war. The ruling passion with the natives is trade, neither Jew or Yankee show more shrewdness in getting the better of a bargain. They tell lies with the same ease, grave and cool assurance, that they do the truth and stick to them with the same obstinacy. If you catch them in a falsehood they are not the least ashamed, but have a come off for all such occasions, and tell you another with such apparent honesty and truth that you are sure to believe them. They show the utmost respect for the dead, and mourn daily at the graves of their friends for three or four months, and sometimes for a year. They keep the graves of their people always clean, even after the towns, where they are located, are deserted or destroyed. The bodies of their kings are embalmed and kept for years before they are buried.

RELIGIOUS BELIEF.

The natives fully believe in a God and an over-ruling Providence that directs all things. It is a common expression with them in speaking of what they intend to do in the future to say "If God helps me."

They have some idea of future rewards and punishments, but what their particular views are is hard to learn.

JUDICIARY.

The king and sometimes other eminent old men act as judge in matters of litigation. Their decision is final—there is no appeal or escape. In cases of fine, where the offender is not worth the money, his friends have to raise it, or he is sold for the amount. Disputes between kings are settled by a grand council, or war. If a native goes to another town and gets credit and does not return to settle his account, any other man coming from the same town is arrested for the amount and has it to pay.

MATRIMONY.

A native wishing to marry a woman for which he has a particular fancy, takes a small present and gives it to the parents of the maid, and tells them what he wants. They open the matter to their daughter, and having obtained her consent, the applicant returns with his money, fifteen dollars in value, puts it into the hands of her parents, and takes his bride home. To get a wife from the royal or noble families costs from one to three hundred dollars. Virginity at marriage may be said to be almost or quite universal among them. The penalty for violating the person of an unmarried female is death inflicted by the hands of women, who beat the wretch to death with sticks, mortar-pestels, &c., in the presence of the whole town.

This law, like all others among them, is so rigidly enforced that it effectually protects their young girls.

Some of the females among the Veys, Golbars, and Mandingoes, are truly handsome. They have finely developed forms, small, handsome feet and hands, round symmetrical limbs, pure snow white teeth, and graceful carriage.

The Vey people have a written language of their own

invention, and many of them who are not acquainted with the English language, are quite conversant with the history of Joseph, Moses, David, and many of the prophets. Such are the natives of Liberia, such are some of their customs and habits. I shall ever remember them as, in many respects, an interesting and kindly race. Some of their worst vices are the result of contact with an unsanctified civilization. Some of their brightest virtues are the native traits of their character unalloyed by civilized vices.

THE END.

Printed by Libri Plureos GmbH in Hamburg, Germany